FULL-STACK WEB DEVELOPMENT MADE PRACTICAL

A Step-by-Step Hands-On Guide from Basic to Advanced for Frontend and Backend Success

© 2024 by Finn Webforge

ABOUT THIS BOOK

Are you ready to master Full-Stack Web Development and build dynamic, scalable, and production-ready web applications? Whether you're starting from scratch or expanding your expertise, this book will guide you step-by-step through every aspect of front-end and back-end development.

From crafting stunning, responsive websites to deploying powerful server-side applications, this book is your one-stop resource for mastering both the foundations and advanced concepts of web development. With a hands-on approach and real-world projects, you'll gain practical skills that are highly relevant in today's tech landscape.

What You'll Learn

HTML, CSS, and Responsive Design: Create visually appealing and mobile-friendly web pages using modern techniques like Grid and Flexbox.

JavaScript Fundamentals: Master the programming language that powers the web, learning DOM manipulation, event handling, and interactivity.

React for Front-End Development: Build dynamic, component-based user interfaces with this powerful library.

Node.js and Express.js: Explore back-end development, including server-side programming and building RESTful APIs.

Database Integration: Store and manage data with MongoDB and SQL, connecting seamlessly with your back-end.

An introduction to Modern Tools: Learn how to use JAMstack and Docker to deploy fast, scalable, and secure applications.

Who Can Use This Book?

This book is designed for:

Beginners who want a structured, step-by-step guide to building a full-stack skillset

Intermediate Developers seeking hands-on projects and deeper knowledge of modern tools and deployment

Professionals looking to stay competitive with an introduction to cutting-edge technologies like Docker and JAMstack.

Why Choose This Book?

Comprehensive Coverage: From front-end foundations to back-end mastery, every aspect of full-stack development is explained in clear, practical steps.

Real-World Projects: Apply your skills by building a portfolio of projects, including a responsive blog page, a To-Do list application, and a full-stack deployment example.

Modern Trends: Gain insights into the latest tools and methodologies used in today's web development industry.

Whether you're aiming to land your first web development job, build your portfolio, or stay ahead in the ever-evolving tech world, this book equips you with the skills to succeed. Let's start building the future of the web—one project at a time!

Bonus: Modern Trends and Tools

Discover (an introduction to) the latest web development technologies, including **JAMstack** and **Docker,** to future-proof your skill set and stay ahead in the ever-evolving tech landscape.

CONTENT

MODULE 1: INTRODUCTION TO FRONT-END DEVELOPMENT

What is Front-End Development?

Overview:

Front-end development, or client-side development, is about building the part of a website or web application that users interact with directly. The primary goal is to create an engaging, seamless user experience by converting data into a graphical interface using HTML, CSS, and JavaScript.

Key Concepts:

- **User Interface (UI):** The visual elements through which users interact with a website, such as buttons, forms, images, and text.

- **User Experience (UX):** The overall feel and experience a user has when interacting with a website. It includes aspects like ease of use, efficiency, and satisfaction.

  Example: Ensuring a form provides clear error message when invalid data is submitted

- **Front-End vs. Back-End:** Front-end development deals with the visual and interactive aspects, that is, it manages what users see and interact with. While back-end development involves server-side operations like databases and application logic.

Tools and Technologies:

1. **HTML (Hypertext Markup Language):** The standard markup language for creating web pages. It structures content on the web.

2. **CSS (Cascading Style Sheets):** The style sheet language used to describe the look and formatting of a document written in HTML.

3. **JavaScript:** A programming language that enables dynamic content and interactivity on websites.

Practical Example: Building a Simple Web Page

1. **Task:**

   Create a simple "About Me" webpage using HTML and CSS.

2. **HTML Structure:**

   Start by creating a basic HTML structure with a `<!DOCTYPE html>`, `<html>`, `<head>`, and `<body>` tags.

   Inside the `<body>`, add a `<header>` with your name as a heading (`<h1>`).

   Add a `<section>` with a short paragraph (`<p>`) describing yourself.

   Include an image (`<img src="your-image-url.jpg" alt="Your Name">`) and a link to your favorite website (`<a href="https://www.example.com">Favorite Site</a>`).

3. **CSS Styling:**

- In the `<head>`, link to an external CSS file or use an internal `<style>` tag.

- Style the header with a background color and center the text.

- Apply margins, padding, and font styles to the paragraph.

- Make the image responsive by setting a max-width and adding a border.

```html
<!DOCTYPE html>

<html lang="en">

<head>

        <meta charset="UTF-8">

        <meta                 name="viewport"
content="width=device-width,              initial-
scale=1.0">

        <title>About Me</title>

        <style>

        body {
```

```css
        font-family: Arial, sans-serif;

        margin: 20px;

        line-height: 1.6;

        }

        header {

        background-color: #4CAF50;

        color: white;

        padding: 10px;

        text-align: center;

        }

        img {

        max-width: 100%;

        height: auto;

        border: 2px solid #ddd;

        }

        p {

        font-size: 1.2em;
```

```
                    }

                </style>

        </head>

        <body>

                <header>

                <h1>Your Name</h1>

                </header>

                <section>

                <p>Hello! I'm [Your Name], and this
        is a brief description about me.</p>

                <img          src="your-image-url.jpg"
        alt="Your Name">

                <p>Check          out          my          <a
        href="https://www.example.com">favorite
        website</a>!</p>

                </section>

        </body>

        </html>
```

4. **Outcome:**

   A simple webpage introducing yourself with basic HTML structure and CSS styling.

Project Setup and Workflow

Overview:

Setting up your development environment and understanding the workflow is essential before starting any project. This includes choosing the right tools, organizing your project files, and using version control to manage your code.

Key Concepts:

- **Development Environment:** The setup of software and tools that developers use to write and test their code. Common tools include text editors like Visual Studio Code, terminal/command-line tools, and version control systems.

- **Version Control with Git:** A system that records changes to a file or set of files over time so that you can recall specific versions later. Git is the most commonly used version control system.

Setting Up the Environment:

1. **Installing VS Code:**

   - Download and install [Visual Studio Code](https://code.visualstudio.com/).

   - Install essential extensions like Emmet, Prettier, and Live Server.

2. **Using the Command Line:**

   - **Navigate Directories:** Learn basic commands like `cd` (change directory), `ls` (list files), and `mkdir` (make directory).

   - **Create a Project Folder:** Open your terminal, navigate to your desired location, and create a new folder using `mkdir my-first-website`.

3. **Version Control with Git:**

   - **Initialize a Repository:** Inside your project folder, run `git init` to initialize a Git repository.

   - **First Commit:** Create a simple `index.html` file, add it to Git with `git add .`, and commit your changes with `git commit -m "Initial commit"`.

Practical Example: Setting Up Your First Project

1. **Task:**

   Create a new project folder and initialize a Git repository.

2. **Steps:**

   - Open the terminal and navigate to your projects directory.

- Run `mkdir my-first-website` to create a new folder.

- Navigate into the folder with `cd my-first-website`.

- Run `git init` to initialize a Git repository.

- Create an `index.html` file and add basic HTML structure.

- Run git add . to stage your files and `git commit -m "Initial commit"` to save your changes.

3. **Outcome:**

A well-organized project with version control set up, ready for development.

Creating Your First Web Page

Overview:

This exercise is designed to help you apply what you've learned by creating a simple web page from scratch. You'll use HTML to structure the content, CSS to style it, and Git to manage your project.

Task:

1. **Create an HTML Page:**

   Build a basic webpage using HTML with a header, a few paragraphs, an image, and a link.

2. **Apply CSS Styling:**

   Style the page using CSS to make it visually appealing. Experiment with colors, fonts, and layouts.

3. **Host on GitHub Pages:**

   Push your project to GitHub and use GitHub Pages to make your site live.

Example Task Implementation:

1. **HTML Structure:**

   Similar to the example provided earlier, but now with more content (additional sections or lists).

2. **CSS Styling:**

   Experiment with different CSS properties like `background-image`, `text-shadow`, and `hover` effects on links.

3. **Deploying the Site:**

   Commit your changes, push them to GitHub, and set up GitHub Pages under the repository settings to host your website.

Expected Outcome:

A polished, web page that introduces basic web development concepts and is live on the web via GitHub Pages.

MODULE 2: HTML AND CSS FOUNDATIONS

Deep Dive into HTML

Overview:

This section provides an in-depth understanding of HTML, the foundational language used to structure web content. You'll learn how to use various HTML elements to create well-organized, semantic web pages.

Key Concepts:

- **HTML Elements (Tags, attributes):** The building block of webpage. They form the structure of web page, wrapped in angle bracket **Example: Tag:** <p> or <hi>; **Attribute:** <p href="https://example.com">Visit Example</p>(This adds a clickable link)

- **Semantic HTML:** The importance of using HTML elements that convey meaning, such as `<header>`, `<footer>`, `<nav>`, `<section>`, and `<article>`.

- **Forms and Input:** Creating forms with various input types for collecting user data.

Practical Example: Building a Multi-Section Web Page

1. **Task:**

   Create a multi-section web page for a fictional company.

2. **HTML Structure:**

   - **Header:** Include the company logo and navigation links.

   - **Main Content:** Create sections for "About Us," "Services," and "Contact Us."

   - **Footer:** Add a footer with social media links and contact information.

3. **Sample Code:**

   ```
   <!DOCTYPE html>
   ```

```html
<html lang="en">

<head>

  <meta charset="UTF-8">

  <meta                    name="viewport"
content="width=device-width, initial-scale=1.0">

  <title>Fictional Company</title>

</head>

<body>

  <header>

    <h1>Fictional Company</h1>

    <nav>

      <ul>

        <li><a       href="#about">About
Us</a></li>

        <li><a
href="#services">Services</a></li>
```

```
            <li><a      href="#contact">Contact
Us</a></li>

        </ul>

    </nav>

</header>

<main>

    <section id="about">

        <h2>About Us</h2>

        <p>Welcome to Fictional Company!
We are dedicated to providing the best
service.</p>

    </section>

    <section id="services">

        <h2>Our Services</h2>

        <ul>

            <li>Web Development</li>
```

```
        <li>Graphic Design</li>

        <li>SEO Optimization</li>

    </ul>

  </section>

  <section id="contact">

    <h2>Contact Us</h2>

    <form>

        <label for="name">Name:</label>

        <input    type="text"    id="name"
name="name">

        <label for="email">Email:</label>

        <input   type="email"   id="email"
name="email">

        <button
type="submit">Submit</button>

    </form>
```

```
        </section>

    </main>

    <footer>

        <p>&copy;          2024          Fictional
Company</p>

        <ul>

            <li><a href="#">Twitter</a></li>

            <li><a
href="#">Facebook</a></li>

            <li><a
href="#">Instagram</a></li>

        </ul>

    </footer>

</body>

</html>
```

4. **Outcome:**

A structured, multi-section webpage that uses semantic HTML to organize content effectively.

Styling with CSS

Overview:

CSS (Cascading Style Sheets) is used to style and layout web pages. This section will cover the basics of CSS, including how to apply styles, manage layouts, and create responsive designs.

Key Concepts:

- **Selectors and Properties:** Understanding how to target HTML elements with CSS and apply various styles.
- **Box Model:** The concept that describes the space an element occupies, including content, padding, border, and margin.
- **Positioning and Layouts:** Techniques for placing elements on a page, including flexbox and grid systems.

Practical Example: Styling the Fictional Company Web Page

1. **Task:**

   Add CSS to style the previously created Fictional Company webpage.

2. **CSS Styling:**
   - Global Styles: Set up basic styles for the body, headings, and links.
   - Layout with Flexbox: Use flexbox to align the navigation menu and sections.
   - Responsive Design: Ensure the page looks good on different screen sizes using media queries.

3. **Sample Code:**

```
body {

font-family: Arial, sans-serif;

line-height: 1.6;

margin: 0;

padding: 0;
```

```css
}


header {

    background-color: #333;

    color: white;

    padding: 10px 0;

    text-align: center;

}


nav ul {

    list-style: none;

    padding: 0;

}


nav ul li {
```

```
        display: inline;

        margin-right: 15px;

    }


nav ul li a {

    color: white;

    text-decoration: none;

}


section {

    padding: 20px;

}


#about {

    background-color: #f4f4f4;
```

```
        }


    #services {

        background-color: #e2e2e2;

    }


    footer {

        background-color: #333;

        color: white;

        text-align: center;

        padding: 10px 0;

        position: fixed;

        bottom: 0;

        width: 100%;

    }
```

```
/* Responsive Design */

@media (max-width: 768px) {

    nav ul li {

        display: block;

        text-align: center;

        margin: 10px 0;

    }

}
```

4. Outcome:

A fully styled and responsive webpage that adjusts layout based on the screen size.

Responsive Web Design

Overview:

Responsive web design ensures that web pages look good on all devices, from desktops to mobile phones. This section focuses on techniques for creating layouts that adapt to different screen sizes.

Key Concepts:

- **Media Queries:** CSS rules that apply styles based on the device's screen size or other characteristics.
- **Fluid Grids:** Layouts that use relative units like percentages instead of fixed units like pixels.
- **Responsive Images:** Techniques to ensure images scale appropriately on different devices.

Practical Example: Making the Fictional Company Page Responsive

1. **Task:**

   Implement responsive design principles to ensure the Fictional Company webpage is mobile-friendly.

2. **Steps:**

    ▪ **Add Media Queries**: Apply different styles for screens wider than 768px and narrower than 768px.

    ▪ **Fluid Grids:** Use percentage-based widths for layout elements like the main content sections.

    ▪ **Responsive Images:** Ensure the company logo and other images scale appropriately.

3. **Sample Code:**

    ...CSS

```css
/* Example Media Query */

@media (max-width: 768px) {

    header {

        text-align: left;

        padding: 15px;

    }
```

```
nav ul {

    display: flex;

    flex-direction: column;

    align-items: center;

}


img {

    max-width: 100%;

    height: auto;

    }

}
```

4. Outcome:

A web page that looks good on both large screens and mobile devices, with images and content that adjust based on the screen size.

Create a Responsive Portfolio Website

Overview:

In this exercise, you'll build a responsive portfolio website from scratch. This project will reinforce your understanding of HTML, CSS, and responsive design principles.

Task:

1. **HTML Structure:**
   - Create a homepage with sections for your profile, projects, and contact information.
   - Use semantic HTML tags to structure your content effectively.

2. **CSS Styling:**
   - Apply global styles, layout techniques, and responsive design principles.
   - Use flexbox or grid layout to create a visually appealing and functional design.

3. **Responsive Design:**
   - Add media queries to adjust the layout and typography for different screen sizes.

- Ensure that images, videos, and other media are responsive.

Example Task Implementation:

1. **HTML Example:**

```html
<section id="profile">

    <h2>About Me</h2>

    <p>I'm a passionate web developer with experience in building responsive and user-friendly websites.</p>

</section>

<section id="projects">

    <h2>My Projects</h2>

    <ul>

        <li>Project 1: <a href="#">E-commerce Website</a></li>
```

```html
        <li>Project   2:   <a   href="#">Portfolio
Website</a></li>

    </ul>

  </section>

  <section id="contact">

    <h2>Contact Me</h2>

    <form>

      <label for="name">Name:</label>

      <input        type="text"        id="name"
name="name">

      <label for="email">Email:</label>

      <input        type="email"        id="email"
name="email">

      <button
type="submit">Submit</button>

    </form>
```

```
</section>
```

2. CSS Example:

```css
body {

    font-family: 'Arial', sans-serif;

    margin: 0;

    padding: 0;

}

#profile, #projects, #contact {

    padding: 20px;

    margin: 20px;

    border: 1px solid #ddd;

}
```

3. Responsive Design:

```css
/* Media Queries for Responsive Design */

@media (max-width: 768px) {

    #profile, #projects, #contact {

        margin: 10px;

        padding: 15px;

        border: none;

        box-shadow: 0 0 10px rgba(0,0,0,0.1);

    }

    h2 {

        font-size: 1.5em;

    }


    p, ul {

        font-size: 1em;
```

```css
}


form {

    display: flex;

    flex-direction: column;

}


input[type="text"], input[type="email"] {

    margin-bottom: 10px;

    padding: 10px;

    font-size: 1em;

    border-radius: 5px;

    border: 1px solid #ccc;

}
```

```
button[type="submit"] {

    padding: 10px;

    background-color: #333;

    color: #fff;

    border: none;

    cursor: pointer;

    border-radius: 5px;

    }

}
```

4. Outcome:

You will have created a responsive portfolio website that not only showcases your skills and projects but also adapts to various screen sizes, ensuring a great user experience across devices.

CSS Grid and Flexbox: Advanced Layout Techniques

Overview:

This section delves into advanced CSS layout techniques using CSS Grid and Flexbox. These tools allow you to create complex and responsive layouts with ease.

Key Concepts:

- **CSS Grid:** A two-dimensional layout system that helps you design layouts by defining rows and columns.

- **Flexbox:** A one-dimensional layout method for arranging elements in a flexible and efficient way, especially useful for creating responsive designs.

Practical Example: Creating a Grid-Based Portfolio Layout

1. **Task:**

   Rebuild your portfolio page using CSS Grid to control the layout of the sections.

2. **Steps:**

   Define a Grid Layout: Use grid-template-columns and grid-template-rows to set up a grid.

   Place Items on the Grid: Use grid-area, grid-column, and grid-row to control the placement of content.

3. **Sample Code:**

```
/* Grid Layout for the Portfolio Page */

.portfolio-container {

    display: grid;

    grid-template-columns: repeat(3, 1fr);

    grid-template-rows: auto;

    gap: 20px;

}
```

```css
.portfolio-item {

    padding: 15px;

    background-color: #f9f9f9;

    border: 1px solid #ddd;

    box-shadow: 0 0 10px rgba(0,0,0,0.1);

}


@media (max-width: 768px) {

    .portfolio-container {

        grid-template-columns: 1fr;

    }

}
```

4. **Outcome:**

A modern, grid-based portfolio layout that scales effectively on different devices, making your portfolio look professional and accessible.

Build a Responsive Blog Page with Flexbox

Overview:

In this exercise, you will create a responsive blog page using Flexbox. This will help you practice arranging elements flexibly and responsively.

Task:

1. **HTML Structure:**

Create a blog page with a navigation bar, a main content area for blog posts, and a sidebar with widgets like recent posts, tags, and categories.

2. **CSS Styling with Flexbox:**
   - Use Flexbox to create a flexible navigation bar and a responsive main content area and sidebar.

- Apply media queries to ensure the layout adjusts on different screen sizes.

3. Sample Code:

```html
<nav class="navbar">
  <ul>
    <li><a href="#">Home</a></li>
    <li><a href="#">About</a></li>
    <li><a href="#">Blog</a></li>
    <li><a href="#">Contact</a></li>
  </ul>
</nav>
<div class="content">
  <main class="blog-posts">
    <article>
```

```html
        <h2>Blog Post Title</h2>

        <p>Content of the blog post...</p>

      </article>

    </main>

    <aside class="sidebar">

      <h3>Recent Posts</h3>

      <ul>

        <li><a href="#">Post 1</a></li>

        <li><a href="#">Post 2</a></li>

        <li><a href="#">Post 3</a></li>

      </ul>

    </aside>

  </div>
```

4. Outcome:

A responsive blog page that uses Flexbox to arrange the navigation, content, and sidebar in a flexible and user-friendly way.

MODULE 3: JAVASCRIPT ESSENTIALS

In this module, we'll explore the fundamental concepts of JavaScript, which is the programming language that adds interactivity to your web pages. By the end of this module, you'll have a solid understanding of JavaScript basics and be able to write simple scripts that enhance the functionality of your websites.

Introduction to JavaScript

Overview:

This section introduces JavaScript, explaining its role in web development and how it integrates with HTML and CSS to create dynamic web pages.

Key Concepts:

- **What is JavaScript?** An overview of JavaScript as a scripting language for the web.
  Example: It powers features like drop-down menu, form validation, live data update etc.

- **Embedding JavaScript:** How to include JavaScript in HTML files using the `<script>` tag.

- **The DOM (Document Object Model):** Understanding how JavaScript interacts with the HTML structure of a webpage.

Practical Example: Embedding JavaScript in an HTML Page

1. **Task:**

   Add a simple JavaScript function to display an alert when a button is clicked.

2. **Steps:**

   - Create an HTML file with a button element.
   - Write a JavaScript function that triggers an alert.
   - Link the function to the button's `onclick` event.

3. **Sample Code:**

   ```
   <!DOCTYPE html>
   ```

```
<html lang="en">

<head>

  <meta charset="UTF-8">

  <meta                    name="viewport"
content="width=device-width, initial-scale=1.0">

  <title>JavaScript Example</title>

</head>

<body>

  <h1>Welcome to My Website</h1>

  <button         onclick="showAlert()">Click
Me!</button>

  <script>

    function showAlert() {

      alert("Button was clicked!");

    }
```

```
</script>

</body>

</html>
```

4. Outcome:

A basic understanding of how to include and run JavaScript within a web page.

JavaScript Syntax and Fundamentals

Overview:

In this section, we'll cover the basics of JavaScript syntax and programming concepts. You'll learn about variables, data types, operators, and control structures.

Key Concepts:

- **Variables and Data Types:** Declaring variables using `var`, `let`, and `const`, and understanding different data types like strings, numbers, and booleans.

- **Operators:** Arithmetic, comparison, and logical operators.
- **Control Structures:** Using `if...else` statements, loops (`for`, `while`), and switch cases to control the flow of the program.

Practical Example: Simple Calculator

1. **Task:**

   Create a simple calculator that performs addition, subtraction, multiplication, and division.

2. **Steps:**
   - Write functions for each operation (addition, subtraction, etc.).
   - Use prompt dialogs to get user input and display the result using alerts.

3. **Sample Code:**

```javascript
function add(a, b) {
```

```
    return a + b;

}

function subtract(a, b) {

    return a - b;

}

function multiply(a, b) {

    return a * b;

}

function divide(a, b) {

    rcturn a / b;

}

let num1 = parseFloat(prompt("Enter the first
number:"));

let num2 = parseFloat(prompt("Enter the
second number:"));
```

```
let operation = prompt("Enter the operation
(+, -, *, /):");

let result;

if (operation === "+") {

    result = add(num1, num2);

} else if (operation === "-") {

    result = subtract(num1, num2);

} else if (operation === "*") {

    result = multiply(num1, num2);

} else if (operation === "/") {

    result = divide(num1, num2);

} else {

    alert("Invalid operation!");

}

alert("The result is: " + result);
```

4. **Outcome:**

A working calculator that performs basic arithmetic operations, reinforcing your understanding of JavaScript fundamentals

Functions and Scope

Overview:

Functions are one of the core building blocks in JavaScript. This section will cover how to define and invoke functions, the concept of scope, and the difference between function declarations and expressions.

Key Concepts:

- **Defining Functions:** How to create reusable blocks of code using functions.
- **Function Expressions:** Storing functions in variables.

- **Scope:** Understanding local and global scope in JavaScript.

Practical Example: Password Validator

1. **Task:**

   Write a function to validate a user's password based on specific criteria (e.g., length, inclusion of numbers).

2. **Steps:**

   - Create a function that checks the length of the password and whether it contains at least one number.
   - Use regular expressions to perform the validation.

3. **Sample Code:**

   ```javascript
   function validatePassword(password) {

       const minLength = 8;
   ```

```
    const hasNumber = /\d/;

    if (password.length < minLength) {

        return "Password must be at least " +
minLength + " characters long.";

    } else if (!hasNumber.test(password)) {

        return "Password must contain at least one
number.";

    } else {

        return "Password is valid.";

    }

  }

  let userPassword = prompt("Enter your
password:");

  alert(validatePassword(userPassword));
```

4. Outcome:

A functional password validator that illustrates how to use functions and handle scope in JavaScript.

Objects and Arrays

Overview:

This section introduces obj ects and arrays, which are essential for storing and manipulating collections of data in JavaScript.

Key Concepts:

- **Objects:** Understanding key-value pairs, creating and accessing object properties.
- **Arrays:** Working with arrays, including methods for adding, removing, and iterating over elements.
- **Manipulating Data:** How to use loops and methods like `map`, `filter`, and `reduce` to work with arrays.

Practical Example: To-Do List Application

1. **Task:**

   Create a simple to-do list application where users can add tasks, mark them as complete, and remove them.

2. **Steps:**

   - Use an array to store the list of tasks.
   - Create functions to add, mark complete, and remove tasks.
   - Use a loop to display the tasks.

3. **Sample Code:**

```javascript
let todoList = [];


function addTask(task) {

    todoList.push({ task: task, completed: false
});

  }
```

```
function completeTask(index) {

    todoList[index].completed = true;

}



function removeTask(index) {

    todoList.splice(index, 1);

}



function displayTasks() {

    todoList.forEach((item, index) => {

    console.log(index + 1 + ". " + item.task +
(item.completed ? " (Completed)" : ""));

    });

}
```

```
addTask("Learn JavaScript");

addTask("Build a website");

completeTask(0);

displayTasks();
```

4. **Outcome:**

A basic to-do list application that demonstrates how to use arrays and objects to manage and display data dynamically.

DOM Manipulation

Overview:

The Document Object Model (DOM) allows JavaScript to interact with and manipulate HTML and

CSS dynamically. This section covers how to select and modify HTML elements using JavaScript.

Key Concepts:

- **Selecting Elements:** How to use `getElementById`, `querySelector`, and other methods to select HTML elements.
- **Manipulating Content:** Changing text, HTML content, and styles using JavaScript.
- **Event Handling:** Attaching event listeners to respond to user interactions like clicks and keypresses.

Practical Example: Interactive Web Page

1. **Task:**

   Enhance your to-do list application by allowing users to interact with the list directly on the web page.

2. **Steps:**

   - Use JavaScript to dynamically create and update HTML elements.

   - Attach event listeners to buttons for adding and removing tasks.

   - Update the DOM in response to user actions.

3. **Sample Code:**

   ```html
   <div>

       <input type="text" id="taskInput" placeholder="Enter a task">

       <button onclick="addTask()">Add Task</button>

   </div>

   <ul id="taskList"></ul>
   ```

```
<script>

    function addTask() {

        const            taskInput         =
document.getElementById("taskInput");

        const            taskList          =
document.getElementById("taskList");

        if (taskInput.value !== "") {

            const li = document.createElement("li");

            li.textContent = taskInput.value;

            taskList.appendChild(li);

            taskInput.value = "";

        }

    }

</script>
```

4. **Outcome:**

An interactive to-do list that allows users to add tasks directly on the webpage, demonstrating DOM manipulation and event handling.

MODULE 4: ADVANCED JAVASCRIPT AND MODERN WEB DEVELOPMENT

This module focuses on more advanced JavaScript concepts and modern practices in web development. You'll learn about asynchronous programming, working with APIs, and using tools like Node.js to handle server-side operations. By the end of this module, you should be able to build dynamic and interactive web applications with complex functionality.

Asynchronous JavaScript - Callbacks, Promises, and Async/Await

Overview:

JavaScript is single-threaded, meaning it can only do one thing at a time. However, modern web applications often require performing multiple operations simultaneously, such as fetching data from a server while allowing the user to interact with the page. This section introduces asynchronous programming in JavaScript, covering callbacks, promises, and the more modern `async/await` syntax.

Key Concepts:

- **Callbacks:** Functions passed as arguments to other functions, which are then executed once a task is completed.
- **Promises:** Objects representing the eventual completion (or failure) of an asynchronous operation.
- **Async/Await:** Syntactic sugar over promises, making asynchronous code look and behave like synchronous code.

Practical Example: Fetching Data from an API

1. **Task:**

   Write a script that fetches data from a public API and displays it on a webpage.

2. **Steps:**

- Use the `fetch` API to retrieve data from an endpoint.
- Handle the response using promises and `async/await`.
- Display the fetched data dynamically on the page.

3. **Sample Code:**

```
async function fetchData() {

    try {

        let response = await fetch('https://jsonplaceholder.typicode.com/posts');

        let data = await response.json();

        displayData(data);

    } catch (error) {

        console.error('Error fetching data:', error);

    }
```

```
    }

    function displayData(posts) {

        const           container           =
document.getElementById('postsContainer');

        posts.forEach(post => {

            let div = document.createElement('div');

            div.className = 'post';

            div.innerHTML                      =
`<h3>${post.title}</h3><p>${post.body}</p
>`;

            containcr.appendChild(div);

        });

    }

    fetchData();
```

4. **Outcome:**

A working example that demonstrates how to fetch and display data asynchronously using `async/await`.

Working with APIs

Overview:

APIs (Application Programming Interfaces) allow different software systems to communicate with each other. This section covers how to consume and interact with APIs using JavaScript, including making GET, POST, PUT, and DELETE requests.

Key Concepts:

- **RESTful APIs:** Understanding REST principles and how to interact with RESTful APIs.

- **CRUD Operations:** Performing Create, Read, Update, and Delete operations via API endpoints.

- **Handling JSON:** Working with JSON (JavaScript Object Notation) for data exchange.

Practical Example: Building a CRUD Application

1. **Task:**

   Create a simple web application that interacts with a RESTful API to perform CRUD operations on a set of data (e.g., a list of users or tasks).

2. **Steps:**

   - Set up a basic HTML structure with forms for adding and updating data, and buttons for deleting entries.

   - Use JavaScript to send requests to the API and handle the responses.

   - Update the DOM based on the results of these requests.

3. **Sample Code:**

```
const                apiUrl                =
'https://jsonplaceholder.typicode.com/users';



// Function to get users

async function getUsers() {

    let response = await fetch(apiUrl);

    let users = await response.json();

    displayUsers(users);

}



// Function to display users

function displayUsers(users) {

    const            userList            =
document.getElementById('userList');

    userList.innerHTML = '';
```

```
    users.forEach(user => {

        let li = document.createElement('li');

        li.textContent        =        `${user.name}
({$user.email})`;

        userList.appendChild(li);

    });

}



    // Call getUsers when the page loads

    window.onload = getUsers;
```

4. Outcome:

A dynamic web application that communicates with an API to perform real-time CRUD operations, illustrating the practical use of JavaScript with APIs.

Introduction to Express.js

Overview:

Express.js is a minimalist web framework for Node.js that simplifies the process of building robust web applications. This section covers the basics of setting up an Express.js application, routing, and handling requests and responses.

Key Concepts:

- **What is Express.js?** An introduction to Express.js and its features.
- **Routing:** How to define routes and handle different HTTP methods (GET, POST, etc.).
- **Middleware:** Understanding middleware and how to use it for tasks like logging, parsing requests, and error handling.

Working with Databases (Optional Extension)

Overview:

This optional section introduces the basics of working with databases in a Node.js environment. You'll learn how to connect to a database, perform CRUD operations, and integrate database functionality into your Express.js applications.

Key Concepts:

- **Database Types:** Understanding SQL vs. NoSQL databases and when to use each.
- **Connecting to a Database:** Using libraries like `Mongoose` for MongoDB or `pg` for PostgreSQL.
- **Performing CRUD Operations:** Implementing database operations (Create, Read, Update, Delete) within an Express.js application.

Practical Example: Connecting to MongoDB

1. **Task:**

   Connect your Express.js application to a MongoDB database and perform CRUD operations on a collection.

2. **Steps:**

   - Install and set up Mongoose to interact with MongoDB.
   - Define a schema and model for your data.
   - Implement routes that interact with the database (e.g., adding and retrieving tasks).

3. **Sample Code:**

```
const mongoose = require('mongoose');



    // Connect to MongoDB

mongoose.connect('mongodb://localhost:27017/
mydatabase', {

    useNewUrlParser: true,

    useUnifiedTopology: true,

});



    // Define a schema for the database
```

```
const taskSchema = new mongoose.Schema({

    name: {

        type: String,

        required: true,

    },

});


// Create a model based on the schema

const Task = mongoose.model('Task',
taskSchema);


// Express.js route to add a new task

app.post('/tasks', async (req, res) => {

    try {
```

```
        const newTask = new Task({ name:
req.body.name });

        await newTask.save();

        res.status(201).json(newTask);

    } catch (err) {

        res.status(400).json({ message: err.message
});

    }

});


// Express.js route to get all tasks

app.get('/tasks', async (req, res) => {

    try {

        const tasks = await Task.find();

        res.json(tasks);
```

```
} catch (err) {

    res.status(500).json({ message: err.message
});

  }

});


// Start the server

app.listen(3000, () => console.log('Server
running on port 3000'));
```

4. Outcome:

You'll have a basic Express.js application connected to a MongoDB database, allowing you to store and retrieve data dynamically. This practical example shows how to integrate database operations into your server-side code, which is essential for building full-stack web applications.

MODULE 5: WEB DEVELOPMENT WITH REACT

This module delves into React, one of the most popular JavaScript libraries for building user interfaces. You'll learn how to create dynamic, responsive web applications using React, focusing on key concepts like components, state management, and routing.

Introduction to React

Overview:

React is a JavaScript library for building user interfaces, developed and maintained by Facebook. It allows developers to create large web applications that can update and render efficiently in response to data changes.

Key Concepts:

- **What is React?** Understanding the basics of React and its place in the web development ecosystem.

- **Components:** The building blocks of a React application.

- **JSX:** A syntax extension that allows you to write HTML directly within JavaScript.

Practical Example: Setting Up Your First React App

1. **Task:**

   Create a simple React application that displays "Hello, World!" on the screen.

2. **Steps:**

   - Install Node.js and npm if you haven't already.

   - Use npx create-react-app to set up a new React project.

   - Modify the App.js file to display "Hello, World!"

3. **Sample Code:**

   ```
   import React from 'react';

   function App() {
   ```

```
    return (

        <div className="App">

            <h1>Hello, World!</h1>

        </div>

    );

}

export default App;
```

4. Outcome:

A basic React application displaying a simple message, giving you a starting point for building more complex interfaces.

React Components and Props

Overview:

Components are the core of any React application. This section will teach you how to create and use components, pass data between them using props, and understand the concept of component hierarchies.

Key Concepts:

- **Functional vs. Class Components:** The difference between functional and class components in React.
- **Props:** Passing data from one component to another.
- **Component Hierarchies:** Organizing components in a parent-child structure.

Practical Example: Creating a Reusable Button Component

1. **Task:**

   Build a reusable button component that can be customized through props.

2. **Steps:**

   - Define a new Button component.

- Use props to customize the text and style of the button.
- Use the button component in your main App component.

3. **Sample Code:**

```
import React from 'react';

function Button({ text, onClick, style }) {

    return (

        <button onClick={onClick} style={style}>

            {text}

        </button>

    );

}

function App() {

    return (

        <div className="App">

            <Button text="Click Me!" onClick={()
=> alert('Button clicked!')} style={{ padding:
```

```
'10px', backgroundColor: 'blue', color: 'white' }}
/>

    </div>

  );

}

export default App;
```

4. Outcome:

A reusable button component that can be used throughout your application, demonstrating how to pass and use props in React.

State Management in React

Overview:

State is what allows React components to change their output over time in response to user interactions, network responses, or anything else. This section covers how to manage state within components, as well as how to update and use state effectively.

Key Concepts:

- **useState Hook:** Managing local state within functional components.
- **State Updates:** Handling state updates and understanding how they trigger re-renders.
- **Complex State:** Working with more complex state objects and arrays.

Practical Example: Building a Counter Component

1. **Task:**

   Create a simple counter that increments and decrements based on user input.

2. **Steps:**

- Use the useState hook to manage the counter's state.

- Implement buttons to increase and decrease the counter value.

- Display the current counter value.

3. **Sample Code:**

```
import React, { useState } from 'react';

function Counter() {

    const [count, setCount] = useState(0);

    return (

      <div>

        <h1>Count: {count}</h1>

        <button onClick={() => setCount(count
+ 1)}>Increment</button>

        <button onClick={() => setCount(count
- 1)}>Decrement</button>

      </div>
```

```
  );

}
```

export default Counter;

4. Outcome:

A functional counter component that demonstrates how to manage and update state within React, providing a clear understanding of how state works in React components.

React Router: Navigating Between Pages

Overview:

Single Page Applications (SPAs) often require navigation between different views or pages without reloading the entire application. React Router is a powerful library that enables this kind of navigation in React applications.

Key Concepts:

- **React Router Basics:** Setting up and using React Router to navigate between different components.

- **Route Parameters:** Passing data through URLs and accessing it in components.

- **Nested Routes:** Structuring routes hierarchically to handle complex navigation structures.

Practical Example: Setting Up a Multi-Page Application

1. **Task:**

   Create a simple multi-page application with a homepage, about page, and contact page.

2. **Steps:**

   - Install React Router using npm.
   - Set up the basic routes using <Route> and <Switch>.

- Create components for each page and link them using <Link>.

3. Sample Code:

```
import React from 'react';

import { BrowserRouter as Router, Route, Switch, Link } from 'react-router-dom';

function Home() {
    return <h1>Home Page</h1>;
}


function About() {
    return <h1>About Page</h1>;
}


function Contact() {
    return <h1>Contact Page</h1>;
}
```

```
function App() {

  return (

    <Router>

      <nav>

        <Link to="/">Home</Link>

        <Link to="/about">About</Link>

        <Link
to="/contact">Contact</Link>

      </nav>

      <Switch>

        <Route        path="/"        exact
component={Home} />

        <Route             path="/about"
component={About} />

        <Route             path="/contact"
component={Contact} />

      </Switch>

    </Router>

  );
```

```
}
```

export default App;

4. Outcome:

A basic multi-page React application with functional navigation, demonstrating how to implement and use React Router for creating SPAs.

Handling Forms in React

Overview:

Forms are an essential part of web applications, allowing users to input data. This section covers how to create and manage forms in React, including how to handle form submissions and validate user input.

Key Concepts:

Controlled Components: Managing form input values through React's state.

Form Validation: Implementing basic form validation using React's state and effects.

Handling Form Submissions: Capturing form data and processing it upon submission.

Practical Example: Building a Simple Signup Form

1. **Task:**

   Create a signup form that captures a user's name, email, and password, and validates the input before submission.

2. **Steps:**
   - Build the form using controlled components.
   - Add basic validation to ensure all fields are filled out.
   - Handle the form submission and display a success message.

3. Sample Code:

```
import React, { useState } from 'react';

function SignupForm() {

  const [formData, setFormData] = useState({
name: ", email: ", password: " });

  const [error, setError] = useState(");


  const handleChange = (e) => {

    const { name, value } = e.target;

    setFormData({ ...formData, [name]: value });

  };

  const handleSubmit = (e) => {

    e.preventDefault();

    if (!formData.name || !formData.email ||
!formData.password) {
```

```
        setError('All fields are required');

    } else {

        setError('');

        alert('Form submitted successfully!');

    }

};



    return (

        <form onSubmit={handleSubmit}>

            <input    type="text"    name="name"
placeholder="Name"    value={formData.name}
onChange={handleChange} />

            <input    type="email"    name="email"
placeholder="Email"    value={formData.email}
onChange={handleChange} />
```

```
        <input              type="password"
name="password"        placeholder="Password"
value={formData.password}
onChange={handleChange} />

        <button              type="submit">Sign
Up</button>

        {error && <p style={{ color: 'red'
}}>{error}</p>}

    </form>

  );

}


export default SignupForm;
```

4. Outcome:

A functional signup form that captures user input and provides validation, giving you hands-on experience with handling forms in React.

MODULE 6: STATE MANAGEMENT AND ADVANCED REACT CONCEPTS

This module will guide you through the more advanced aspects of React, particularly focusing on state management and how to handle complex data flows within your application. By the end of this module, you'll be proficient in using state management tools like Redux and the Context API, and you'll also learn techniques to optimize React applications for better performance.

Introduction to State Management

Overview:

State management is a crucial aspect of any React application, especially as applications grow in complexity. While React's built-in state mechanism works well for simple applications, managing state across multiple components can become challenging in larger applications. This section introduces the concept of global state management.

Key Concepts:

- **Local vs. Global State:** Understanding when to lift state and why global state management is necessary.

- **Common State Management Libraries:** An overview of popular state management libraries like Redux, MobX, and the Context API.

- **Choosing the Right Tool:** When and why to use different state management solutions.

Practical Example: Refactoring an App to Use Global State

1. **Task:**

   Convert an application that uses local state across multiple components into one that uses global state.

2. **Steps:**
   - Identify the components sharing state.
   - Implement the Context API to manage this state globally.

- Refactor the components to use the global state instead of local state.

3. Sample Code:

```
import React, { createContext, useState, useContext } from 'react';

const GlobalStateContext = createContext();

function GlobalStateProvider({ children }) {

    const [state, setState] = useState({ theme: 'light', user: null });

    return (

        <GlobalStateContext.Provider value={[state, setState]}>

            {children}
        </GlobalStateContext.Provider>
    );
}
```

```
function App() {

  return (

    <GlobalStateProvider>

      <Navbar />

      <UserProfile />

    </GlobalStateProvider>

  );

}


function Navbar() {

  const [state] = useContext(GlobalStateContext);

  return <nav>Theme: {state.theme}</nav>;

}

function UserProfile() {

  const [state, setState] = useContext(GlobalStateContext);
```

```
return (

  <div>

    <p>User: {state.user ? state.user.name :
'Guest'}</p>

    <button   onClick={()   =>   setState({
...state, user: { name: 'John Doe' } })}>

      Login

    </button>

  </div>

);

}

export default App;
```

4. Outcome:

A refactored application that uses global state, showcasing how to manage state across different components effectively using the Context API.

Deep Dive into Redux

Overview:

Redux is a predictable state container for JavaScript apps, often used with React. It helps you manage your application state in a more organized and maintainable way, especially as the app grows. This section will cover the fundamentals of Redux, including actions, reducers, and the store.

Key Concepts:

- **Redux Architecture:** Understanding the core concepts of Redox—store, actions, reducers, and how they interact.
- **Setting Up Redux:** How to integrate Redux into a React application.
- **Connecting Components to Redux:** Using `connect` and `useSelector` to access the Redux state in your components.

Practical Example: Implementing a Redux Store

1. **Task:**

   Set up Redux in an existing React application to manage a simple counter state.

2. **Steps:**

   - Install Redux and `react-redux` libraries.
   - Create actions and reducers to handle the counter state.
   - Configure the Redux store and connect it to your application.

3. **Sample Code:**

```
import { createStore } from 'redux';

import { Provider, useSelector, useDispatch } from 'react-redux';




// Actions

const increment = () => ({ type: 'INCREMENT' });
```

```
const decrement = () => ({ type:
'DECREMENT' });



// Reducer

function counterReducer(state = { count: 0
}, action) {

  switch (action.type) {

    case 'INCREMENT':

      return { count: state.count + 1 };

    case 'DECREMENT':

      return { count: state.count - 1 };

    default:

      return state;

  }

}
```

```
// Store

const store = createStore(counterReducer);

function Counter() {

  const count = useSelector(state =>
state.count);

  const dispatch = useDispatch();



  return (

    <div>

      <h1>{count}</h1>

      <button onClick={() =>
dispatch(increment())}>Increment</button>

      <button onClick={() =>
dispatch(decrement())}>Decrement</button
>
```

```
        </div>

    );

}

function App() {

    return (

        <Provider store={store}>

            <Counter />

        </Provider>

    );

}

export default App;
```

4. Outcome:

A React application integrated with Redux to manage a simple counter, demonstrating the process of setting up Redux and connecting components to the Redux store.

Advanced State Management with Redux

Overview:

Once you've mastered the basics of Redux, it's time to explore more advanced topics, such as handling asynchronous operations, using middleware, and structuring a large-scale Redux application.

Key Concepts:

- **Redux Middleware:** How middleware like `redux-thunk` and `redux-saga` can be used to handle side effects and asynchronous actions in Redux.

- **Asynchronous Actions:** Dispatching actions that involve API calls and managing the resulting state.

- **Optimizing Redux Applications:** Techniques for improving performance and maintainability in large Redux applications.

Practical Example: Fetching Data from an API with Redux Thunk

1. **Task:**

   Implement an asynchronous action in Redux to fetch data from an API and store it in the Redux state.

2. **Steps:**
   - Install `redux-thunk` and apply it as middleware in your Redux store.
   - Create an action that fetches data from an API and dispatches the result.
   - Update the reducer to handle the fetched data.

3. **Sample Code:**

   ```
   import { createStore, applyMiddleware } from 'redux';

   import thunk from 'redux-thunk';

   import { Provider, useDispatch, useSelector } from 'react-redux';
   ```

```
import axios from 'axios';



// Actions

const fetchDataSuccess = (data) => ({ type:
'FETCH_DATA_SUCCESS', payload: data });


const fetchData = () => {

  return async (dispatch) => {

    const response = await
axios.get('https://api.example.com/data');

    dispatch(fetchDataSuccess(response.data));

  };

};

// Reducer

function dataReducer(state = { data: [] },
action) {
```

```
        switch (action.type) {

          case 'FETCH_DATA_SUCCESS':

            return { ...state, data: action.payload };

          default:

            return state;

        }

    }


    // Store

    const store = createStore(dataReducer,
applyMiddleware(thunk));


    function DataComponent() {

      const dispatch = useDispatch();

      const data = useSelector(state => state.data);
```

```
useEffect(() => {

    dispatch(fetchData());

}, [dispatch]);



return (

    <div>

        <h1>Data from API</h1>

        <ul>

            {data.map(item => <li
key={item.id}>{item.name}</li>)}

        </ul>

    </div>

);

}
```

```
function App() {

    return (

        <Provider store={store}>

            <DataComponent />

        </Provider>

    );

}

export default App;
```

4. Outcome:

A Redux-based React application that fetches data from an API and manages the fetched data within the Redux state, illustrating the use of middleware for handling asynchronous operations.

Optimizing React Applications

Overview:

As your React applications grow in size and complexity, performance optimization becomes increasingly important. This section will cover techniques and best practices for optimizing React applications.

Key Concepts:

- **Code Splitting:** Using tools like `React.lazy` and `Suspense` to split your code and load components only when they're needed.
- **Memoization:** Preventing unnecessary re-renders with `React.memo` and `useMemo`.
- **Performance Monitoring:** Using tools like React DevTools and Lighthouse to measure and improve performance.

Practical Example: Implementing Code Splitting**

1. **Task:**

   Implement code splitting in a React application to load components only when they are needed.

2. **Steps:**

   - Use `React.lazy` to dynamically import components.
   - Wrap the lazy-loaded components with `Suspense` to handle loading states.
   - Measure the impact on performance using React DevTools.

3. **Sample Code:**

```
import React, { Suspense } from 'react';
```

```
const HeavyComponent = React.lazy(() =>
import('./HeavyComponent'));
```

```
function App() {
```

```
    return (

        <div className="App">

            <Suspense
fallback={<div>Loading...</div>}>

                <HeavyComponent />

            </Suspense>

        </div>

    );

}

    export default App;
```

4. Outcome:

A React application that leverages code splitting to improve load times and overall performance, showcasing the benefits of loading components only when they are needed.

MODULE 7: INTRODUCTION TO BACK-END DEVELOPMENT

Module 7 marks the transition from front-end to back-end development. You'll start learning about the server-side of web applications, focusing on how to build, manage, and optimize servers, databases, and APIs. By the end of this module, you'll have a solid foundation in back-end technologies, preparing you for full-stack development.

Back-End Development

Overview:

Back-end development involves building and maintaining the server, database, and application logic that power a web application. This section provides an introduction to the key concepts and technologies involved in back-end development.

Key Concepts:

Client-Server Architecture: Understanding how clients and servers interact over the internet.

Server-Side Programming Languages: An overview of popular server-side languages like Node.js, Python, and Ruby.

APIs: Understanding RESTful APIs and how they facilitate communication between the client and server.

Databases: Introduction to SQL and NoSQL databases, including how they store and retrieve data.

Practical Example: Setting Up a Simple Node.js Server

1. **Task:**

   Set up a basic Node.js server that responds with "Hello, World!" to incoming HTTP requests.

2. **Steps:**

   - Install Node.js and set up a new project.
   - Create a simple server using the `http` module.

- Run the server and test it with a web browser or Postman.

3. Sample Code:

```
const http = require('http');

const server = http.createServer((req, res) => {

    res.statusCode = 200;

    res.setHeader('Content-Type', 'text/plain');

    res.end('Hello, World!\n');

});

server.listen(3000, () => {

    console.log('Server          running          at
http://127.0.0.1:3000/');

});
```

4. Outcome:

A basic understanding of how to create a server with Node.js, laying the groundwork for more complex back-end tasks.

Introduction to Node.js and Express

Overview:

Node.js is a JavaScript runtime that allows you to run JavaScript on the server side, while Express is a popular web framework for Node.js that simplifies the process of building web applications and APIs. This section covers the basics of setting up a Node.js environment and creating a simple Express application.

Key Concepts:

Node.js Fundamentals: Understanding the event-driven, non-blocking I/O model that powers Node.js.

Express.js Basics: Introduction to routing, middleware, and handling HTTP requests and responses with Express.

Practical Example: Building a Simple Express Application

1. **Task:**

   Build a basic Express application that handles different routes and serves static files.

2. **Steps:**

   - Install Express and set up a basic application structure.
   - Create routes for different pages (e.g., home, about, contact).
   - Serve static files (e.g., CSS, images) using Express.

3. **Sample Code:**

```
const express = require('express');

const path = require('path');
```

```
const app = express();


app.get('/', (req, res) => {

    res.send('Welcome to the Home Page');

});


app.get('/about', (req, res) => {

    res.send('About Us');

});


app.use('/static',
express.static(path.join(__dirname, 'public')));


app.listen(3000, () => {
```

```
        console.log('Server    is    running    on
http://localhost:3000');

    });
```

4. Outcome:

A simple Express application that handles routing and serves static files, providing a foundation for more advanced Express.js features.

Working with Databases: MongoDB and Mongoose

Overview:

Databases are essential for storing and retrieving data in web applications. This section introduces MongoDB, a popular NoSQL database, and Mongoose, an ODM (Object Data Modeling) library for MongoDB and Node.js. You'll learn how to connect to a MongoDB database, define schemas, and perform CRUD (Create, Read, Update, Delete) operations.

Key Concepts:

- **NoSQL Databases:** Understanding the differences between SQL and NoSQL databases, and why MongoDB is commonly used in modern web applications.
- **MongoDB Basics:** How to set up a MongoDB database and perform basic operations.
- **Mongoose:** Using Mongoose to create schemas, models, and interact with MongoDB.

Practical Example: Creating a RESTful API with MongoDB and Mongoose

1. **Task:**

   Build a simple RESTful API using Express, MongoDB, and Mongoose.

2. **Steps:**

   - Set up MongoDB and connect it to your Express application using Mongoose.

   - Define a Mongoose schema and model for a basic resource (e.g., a product).

   - Implement CRUD routes in Express for creating, reading, updating, and deleting the resource.

3. Sample Code:

```javascript
const express = require('express');

const mongoose = require('mongoose');



mongoose.connect('mongodb://localhost/mydatabase', { useNewUrlParser: true, useUnifiedTopology: true });
```

```
const        productSchema        =        new
mongoose.Schema({

    name: String,

    price: Number,

});


const Product = mongoose.model('Product',
productSchema);


const app = express();

app.use(express.json());


app.post('/products', async (req, res) => {

    const product = new Product(req.body);

    await product.save();
```

```
        res.status(201).send(product);

});


app.get('/products', async (req, res) => {

    const products = await Product.find();

    res.send(products);

});


app.put('/products/:id', async (req, res) => {

    const       product      =        await
Product.findByIdAndUpdate(req.params.id,
req.body, { new: true });

    res.send(product);

});
```

```
app.delete('/products/:id', async (req, res) => {

    await
Product.findByIdAndDelete(req.params.id);

    res.send({ message: 'Product deleted' });

});



app.listen(3000, () => {

    console.log('Server          running          on
http://localhost:3000');

});
```

4. **Outcome:**

A functional RESTful API built with Express, MongoDB, and Mongoose, demonstrating how to perform CRUD operations and manage data in a NoSQL database.

Authentication and Security

Overview:

Security is a critical aspect of web development, especially when handling user data. This section covers how to implement authentication in your Node.js application, including best practices for securing user data and protecting your application from common security threats.

Key Concepts:

- **Authentication vs. Authorization:** Understanding the difference and how to implement both.
- **JSON Web Tokens (JWT):** Using JWT for secure token-based authentication.
- **Security Best Practices:** Techniques to protect your application from common vulnerabilities like SQL injection, XSS, and CSRF.

Practical   Example: Implementing   JWT
Authentication

1. **Task:**

Implement JWT-based authentication in an
Express application.

2. **Steps:**

   - Set up user registration and login routes.
   - Generate and validate JWT tokens for
     authenticated routes.
   - Protect sensitive routes using middleware to
     verify the JWT.

3. **Sample Code:**

```
const express = require('express');

const jwt = require('jsonwebtoken');

const bcrypt = require('bcryptjs');
```

```
const users = []; // This would normally be a database


const app = express();

app.use(express.json());


app.post('/register', async (req, res) => {

    const hashedPassword = await bcrypt.hash(req.body.password, 10);

    const user = { name: req.body.name, password: hashedPassword };

    users.push(user);

    res.status(201).send('User registered');

});


app.post('/login', async (req, res) => {
```

```
const user = users.find(u => u.name ===
req.body.name);

if (user && await
bcrypt.compare(req.body.password,
user.password)) {

const token = jwt.sign({ name: user.name
}, 'secretkey');

res.json({ token });

} else {

res.status(400).send('Invalid credentials');

}

});


function authenticateToken(req, res, next) {

const token =
req.headers['authorization']?.split(' ')[1];
```

```
        if (!token) return res.sendStatus(401);


        jwt.verify(token, 'secretkey', (err, user) => {

            if (err) return res.sendStatus(403);

            req.user = user;

            next();

        });

    }


    app.get('/protected', authenticateToken, (req,
res) => {

        res.send('This is a protected route');

    });


    app.listen(3000, () => {
```

```
        console.log('Server        running        on
http://localhost:3000');

    });
```

4. Outcome:

A Node.js application with secure JWT-based authentication, illustrating how to protect routes and manage user sessions securely.

MODULE 8: FULL-STACK INTEGRATION AND DEPLOYMENT

Module 8 brings everything together by integrating front-end and back-end components into a full-stack web application. You'll learn how to connect your front-end with your back-end, implement full-stack features, and deploy your application to a production environment. This final module is where all your skills converge, culminating in a deployable web application.

Integrating Front-End with Back-End

Overview:

Integrating the front-end and back-end of your web application involves connecting the client-side interface with server-side logic and databases. This section covers how to build a cohesive application by linking your front-end (HTML, CSS, JavaScript) with your back-end (Node.js, Express, MongoDB).

Key Concepts:

- **API Integration:** How to use AJAX or Fetch API to communicate with your back-end server.
- **Routing:** Managing routes and handling client requests in a full-stack environment.
- **Data Flow:** Understanding how data moves between the front-end and back-end.

Practical Example: Building a Full-Stack To-Do App

1. **Task:**

   Create a full-stack To-Do application where users can add, view, update, and delete tasks.

2. **Steps:**
   - **Front-End:** Create a simple interface using HTML, CSS, and JavaScript.
   - **Back-End:** Set up routes in Express to handle CRUD operations.

- **Integration:** Use Fetch API to communicate between the front-end and back-end, updating the UI based on server responses.

3. **Sample Code:**

Front-End:

```
<input        type="text"        id="taskInput"
placeholder="Enter a new task">

<button              onclick="addTask()">Add
Task</button>

<ul id="taskList"></ul>


<script>

    async function addTask() {

        const            task            =
document.getElementById('taskInput').value;

        const response = await fetch('/tasks', {
```

```javascript
      method: 'POST',

      headers:        {         'Content-Type':
'application/json' },

      body: JSON.stringify({ task })

    });

    const newTask = await response.json();


document.getElementById('taskList').innerHTML
+= `<li>${newTask.task}</li>`;

    }

  </script>
```

Back-End:

```javascript
const express = require('express');

const app = express();
```

```
app.use(express.json());


let tasks = [];


app.post('/tasks', (req, res) => {

    const task = { id: tasks.length + 1, task:
req.body.task };

    tasks.push(task);

    res.status(201).json(task);

});


app.listen(3000, () => {

    console.log('Server          running          on
http://localhost:3000');

});
```

4. **Outcome:**

A simple yet complete full-stack To-Do app that demonstrates how to connect a front-end interface with a back-end server.

Full-Stack Features: Authentication and State Management

Overview:

Adding advanced features like authentication and state management to your full-stack application enhances user experience and security. This section focuses on integrating user authentication and managing application state across different parts of your app.

Key Concepts:

- **Authentication Flows:** Implementing secure sign-up, login, and logout functionalities.
- **State Management:** Managing user data, session states, and application state using tools

like Redux (for front-end) and session management (for back-end).

Practical Example: Implementing Full-Stack User Authentication

1. **Task:**

   Extend the To-Do app to include user authentication so that tasks are specific to each user.

2. **Steps:**

   - **Front-End:** Create login and registration forms, manage session tokens with local storage or cookies.
   - **Back-End:** Implement routes for user registration, login, and token-based authentication using JWT.

3. **Sample Code:**

   Front-End:

   ```
   <form id="loginForm">
   ```

```
    <input      type="text"      id="username"
placeholder="Username">

    <input   type="password"   id="password"
placeholder="Password">

    <button                     type="button"
onclick="login()">Login</button>

    </form>



    <script>

    async function login() {

        const            username            =
document.getElementById('username').value;

        const            password            =
document.getElementById('password').value;

        const response = await fetch('/login', {

        method: 'POST',
```

```
        headers:        {        'Content-Type':
'application/json' },

        body:    JSON.stringify({    username,
password })

    });

    const data = await response.json();

    if (data.token) {

        localStorage.setItem('token',
data.token);

        }

    }

  </script>
```

Back-End:

```
const express = require('express');

const jwt = require('jsonwebtoken');
```

```
const bcrypt = require('bcryptjs');



const users = []; // This would be a database
in a real app



app.post('/register', async (req, res) => {

    const hashedPassword = await
bcrypt.hash(req.body.password, 10);

    const user = { username:
req.body.username, password: hashedPassword };

    users.push(user);

    res.status(201).send('User registered');

});



app.post('/login', async (req, res) => {
```

```
        const user = users.find(u => u.username
=== req.body.username);

        if        (user        &&        await
bcrypt.compare(req.body.password,
user.password)) {

            const token = jwt.sign({ username:
user.username }, 'secret');

            res.json({ token });

        } else {

            res.status(400).send('Invalid credentials');

        }

    });
```

4. **Outcome:**

An extended full-stack application that supports user authentication, demonstrating how to handle user-specific data and secure routes.

Deployment to Production

Overview:

Once your application is complete, it's time to deploy it to a production environment where users can access it online. This section covers the deployment process, including setting up hosting, configuring a production server, and ensuring your app runs smoothly in a live environment.

Key Concepts:

- **Hosting Services:** Overview of popular hosting platforms like Heroku, Vercel, and AWS.
- **CI/CD Pipelines:** Automating the deployment process using continuous integration and continuous deployment tools.
- **Environment Variables:** Managing sensitive information like API keys and database credentials securely.

Practical Example: Deploying the To-Do App to Heroku

1. **Task:**

   Deploy the full-stack To-Do app to Heroku, making it accessible to users on the web.

2. **Steps:**

   - Set Up Heroku: Install the Heroku CLI, create a new Heroku app, and configure your environment.
   - Prepare for Deployment: Set up a `Procfile`, manage environment variables, and connect your Git repository.
   - Deploy and Test: Push your code to Heroku and test your live application.

3. **Sample Code:**

Procfile (for Node.js):

```
web: node index.js
```

Deploy Command:

```
git add .
```

git commit -m "Prepare for deployment"

git push heroku master

4. **Outcome:**

A fully deployed application accessible on the web, demonstrating how to take your development project from local to global.

Review and Summary of Module 8

Module 8 brings together everything you've learned throughout the course, integrating front-end and back-end development into a full-stack application. You've learned how to connect the two sides of a web application, implement full-stack features, and deploy your project to a live environment, equipping you with the skills to build and launch complete web applications.

BONUS:

INTRODUCTION TO **JAMstack** AND **Docker**

A MODERN TRENDS AND ADVANCED
TOOLS IN WEB DEVELOPMENT

JAMstack

Overview:

JAMstack is a modern web development architecture focused on better performance, higher security, and scalability. It decouples the front-end from the back-end, relying on JavaScript, APIs, and Markup for building fast and responsive applications.

Key Concepts:

- **JavaScript:** Used for dynamic functionality on the front-end.
- **APIs:** Server-side operations are handled via APIs, such as for handling database queries, authentication, or payments.
- **Markup:** HTML is pre-built during deployment and served as static files.

Advantages:

1. **Improved Performance:** Since most content is served as static files through a Content Delivery

Network (CDN), load times are significantly reduced.

2. **Enhanced Security:** By minimizing server-side dependencies and directly serving static files, the security risk from attacks is reduced.

3. **Scalability:** Static files can be easily scaled to handle large numbers of users.

Tools for JAMstack:

1. **Next.js:** A popular React-based framework that allows for server-side rendering, static generation, and dynamic routing.

2. **Gatsby:** A React framework that helps in building super-fast static websites by compiling pages into static files.

3. **Netlify:** A platform that integrates well with JAMstack architectures, offering continuous deployment and automatic scaling.

Practical Example: Building a Static Blog with Next.js

Step 1: Set up a new Next.js Project

```bash
npx create-next-app@latest my-static-blog

cd my-static-blog

npm run dev
```

Step 2: Create a Simple Blog Page

1. Create a file called `pages/index.js`.
2. Add content that will be rendered as HTML:

```javascript
export default function Home() {

  return (

    <div>
```

```
<h1>Welcome to My Blog</h1>

<p>This is a blog about JAMstack
development.</p>

</div>

);

}
```

Step 3: Deploy the Blog on Netlify

Connect the GitHub repository to Netlify for easy continuous deployment and scaling.

Docker: for Development and Deployment

Overview:

Docker is a tool designed to make it easier to create, deploy, and run applications by using containers. Containers are lightweight, standalone, and executable packages that contain everything needed to run an application: code, runtime, libraries, and system settings.

Why Use Docker?

1. **Environment Consistency:** Docker ensures that your app runs identically in different environments (local, staging, production).

2. **Simplified Deployment:** Docker allows developers to package their entire application (including dependencies) into a container, which can be deployed to any server running Docker.

3. **Scalability:** Docker containers can be easily scaled and deployed across multiple servers.

Key Concepts:

- **Dockerfile:** A script containing a series of commands to assemble an image, which serves as the base of the container.

- **Image:** A snapshot of an application at a particular state. Once created, it can be used to create a container.

- **Container:** A running instance of a Docker image, which is isolated from other containers and the host environment.

Practical Example: Containerizing a Node.js App with Docker

Step 1: Write a Simple Node.js Application

- Create a new directory and a file called `app.js`:

    ```javascript
    const http = require('http');
    ```

```
const port = 3000;

const requestHandler = (req, res) => {

  res.end('Hello from Docker!');

};


const              server              =
http.createServer(requestHandler);


server.listen(port, () => {

  console.log(`Server is running on port
${port}`);

});
```

- Create a `package.json` file for your app:

    ```json
    {

      "name": "docker-node-app",

      "version": "1.0.0",

      "main": "app.js",
```

```json
    "dependencies": {
      "http": "*"
    },
    "scripts": {
      "start": "node app.js"
    }
  }
```

Step 2: Create a Dockerfile

In the same directory as your Node.js app, create a `Dockerfile`:

```dockerfile
FROM node:14

WORKDIR /app

COPY package*.json ./

RUN npm install
```

COPY . .

CMD ["npm", "start"]

Step 3: Build and Run the Docker Container

Build the Docker image:

```bash
docker build -t my-node-app .
```

Run the container:

```bash
docker run -p 3000:3000 my-node-app
```

"Visit `http://localhost:3000` in your browser to see "Hello from Docker!" displayed, showing that your app is running inside a Docker container."

Docker Deployment:

- **Heroku:** Docker containers can be deployed to Heroku for web hosting.
- **DigitalOcean:** You can deploy Docker containers directly on virtual servers or droplets using Docker Compose for easy scaling.

Summary/Conclusion

This bonus, covering modern tools like, **JAMstack** and **Docker** introduces you to current web development trends. They reflect the shift towards lightweight, modular architectures that are easy to deploy and scale, aligning with modern development practices.